The Budding Artist

Edited by Laura Laxton
Illustrations by Kathi Dery

Acknowledgments

The following individuals contributed ideas and activities to this book:

A. Gail Whitney, Ann Gudowski, Audrey F. Kanoff, Barbara J. Lindsay, Barbara Saul, Carol Nelson, Cory McIntyre, Dani Rosensteel, Jean Potter, Kaethe Lewandowski, Leslie B. Brunner, Linda Atamian, Linda S. Andrews, Lisa M. Chichester, Mary Jo Shannon, Mary Rozum Anderson, MaryAnn F. Kohl, Michelle Barnea, Mike Krestar, Nancy Gardner, Nicole Sparks, Pam Shelest, Penni Smith, Rebecca McMahon, Sandra Fisher, Sandra Gratias, Sandra Hutchins Lucas, Sandra L. Nagel, Susan Oldham Hill, Teresa J. Nos, Tina R. Woehler, Valerie Chellew, Virginia Jean Herrod

THE *Budding* ARTIST

EDITED BY LAURA LAXTON

ILLUSTRATIONS BY KATHI DERY

Gryphon House, Inc.
LEWISVILLE, NC

Published by Gryphon House, Inc.
PO Box 10, Lewisville, NC 27023
800.638.0928; 877.638.7576 (fax)

Visit us on the web at www.gryphonhouse.com.

Cover illustration courtesy of Hannah Minney for iStock Photography.

Library of Congress Cataloging-in-Publication Data
The budding artist / edited by Gryphon House ; illustrations by Kathi Dery.
    pages cm – (The budding series)
ISBN 978-0-87659-384-4 (pbk.)
1. Art–Juvenile literature. 2. Creative activities and seat work–Juvenile literature. I. Dery, K. Whelan, illustrator.
N7440.B83 2012
702.8–dc23
                            2011049432

Bulk Purchase
Gryphon House books are available for special premiums and sales promotions as well as for fund-raising use. Special editions or book excerpts also can be created to specifications. For details, contact the Director of Marketing at Gryphon House.

Disclaimer
Gryphon House, Inc. cannot be held responsible for damage, mishap, or injury incurred during the use of or because of activities in this book. Appropriate and reasonable caution and adult supervision of children involved in activities and corresponding to the age and capability of each child involved is recommended at all times. Do not leave children unattended at any time. Observe safety and caution at all times.

Table of Contents

CHAPTER 4: Nuts About Nature

CHAPTER 5: Create with Color

CHAPTER 6: Masterpieces and More

Recommended Books

The children's books listed in "Books to Enjoy" may include books that are currently out of print. These books can be purchased used or are most likely available in your local library.

To the Parents of Budding Artists

Creating art is as much about the journey as it is about the finished product.

The ideas in this book will get your young child excited about the process of creating. He can explore painting with branches or string or magnets. She can sculpt something from playdough or simply enjoy the experience of squishing clay. He can make glue glow and sparkle. She can see what happens when paint touches raindrops or ice.

Expand your child's artistic horizons by branching out and experimenting with a variety of media. Your child will enjoy doing many of the activities independently, but the ideas in this book provide wonderful opportunities to spend time with your child as you create something together. Enjoy the delight and wonder your child feels at all his discoveries. And save lots of room on the fridge and the bulletin board—you have a budding artist on your hands!

☑ **Tip:** Budding artists can be enthusiastic (and not always careful) when they are creating their masterpieces. Use paint smocks or old shirts to protect their clothing.

CHAPTER I

Chalk, Crayons, and Crystals, Oh My!

Create Custom Chalk

Create your custom colors and make your mark!

What You'll Need

measuring spoons

paper cups

plaster of Paris

powdered tempera paint, various colors

tongue depressors or craft sticks

2 tablespoons water

Books to Enjoy

The Art Lesson by Tomie dePaola

Chalk by Bill Thomson

A Piece of Chalk by Jennifer A. Ericsson

The Red Chalk by Iris van der Heide

What to Do

1 Use a tongue depressor to mix 1 tablespoon tempera paint and 1 tablespoon water in a paper cup, stirring until the mixture is smooth.

2 Add 2 tablespoons plaster of Paris, and continue stirring. (If necessary, add additional plaster of Paris until the solution is creamy.)

3 Leave the tongue depressor in the cup to use as a handle.

4 Repeat steps 1–3 to make additional colors.

5 Locate a safe spot where the mixture won't be disturbed as it hardens. Carry the cup(s) to that location.

6 Allow the mixture to dry overnight or until it is very hard (about six hours).

7 Peel—or even rip!—off the paper cup. Go outside, and draw pictures using the chalk!

Try This!

Use the chalk to practice writing your name, letters, and numbers.

10

Chalk-Scraping Prints

The same chalk dust that leaves smudges all over your clothes and hands can make swirly art prints. This activity is a good way to use up small and broken pieces of chalk.

What You'll Need

children's safety scissors

different colors of chalk
(sidewalk chalk works best)

newspapers

shallow pan of water

white paper (cut into shapes, if desired)

Books to Enjoy

A Piece of Chalk
by Jennifer Ericsson

Sidewalk Chalk: Poems of the City
by Carole Boston Weatherford

What to Do

1. Prepare the area by spreading out newspapers, then fill the shallow pan with water.

2. Hold chalk over the water, and scrape it with scissors to create chalk dust, which will float on top of the water. (You may need adult help and guidance.)

3. Scrape the chalk until you have many colors of chalk dust floating on top of the water. Three or four colors usually make a pretty print.

4. Hold the paper, and place it gently on top of the water. Do not push it under!

5. Grasp two corners, and pick the paper up carefully. Look at the print. What happened? How did the chalk transfer from water to paper? Did the colors mingle at all, or did they overlap? How is the look created by chalk dust different from what paint would do?

6. Allow the print to dry. If you want to make more prints, you may need to scrape more chalk dust onto the surface of the water. (You may be able to make four or five prints before you need to change the water because it is filled with chalk dust. The dust drops to the bottom of the pan when you make a print.)

shallow pan of water

newspapers

white paper

different shapes

children's safety scissors

sidewalk chalk

Fingerprint Creatures

Your fingerprint creations will be as unique as you are!

What You'll Need

paper

pen or pencil

washable-ink pads

Books to Enjoy

Ed Emberley's Complete Funprint Drawing Book by Ed Emberley

Ed Emberley's Drawing Book of Faces by Ed Emberley

Ed Emberley's Great Thumbprint Drawing Book by Ed Emberley

I Wish I Were a Butterfly by James Howe

The Very Busy Spider by Eric Carle

The Very Hungry Caterpillar by Eric Carle

What to Do

1. Set out the ink pads and paper, and use one finger to make fingerprints on the paper.
2. Think about the kinds of creatures that you could make from these fingerprints. For example, five or six fingerprints together form a caterpillar; four fingerprints form the wings of a butterfly; one fingerprint with legs makes a spider.
3. Use a pen or pencil to draw the details, such as legs and eyes.
4. Fire up your pointer finger, and see what else you can make!

bird · sun · butterfly · tree · spider · caterpillar · dog

Try This!

Make up a story about your drawings.

Jack Frost Pictures

Snow sparkling in the sunlight makes us think of fun cold-weather activities, such as sledding and building snowmen. With this technique, you can make sparkling winter scenes no matter what the weather!

What You'll Need

dark construction paper

Epsom salt

jar

paint cup

paintbrushes

warm water

Books to Enjoy

One Winter's Day
by M. Christina Butler

Winter Is the Warmest Season
by Lauren Stringer

What to Do

1. Put equal amounts of warm water and Epsom salt into a jar, and then stir the mixture until the Epsom salt dissolves.
2. Pour the mixture into a paint cup. (You may need adult help or guidance with this step.)
3. Paint a design on the dark paper with the Epsom-salt solution. What are you painting? Is it an object or a scene? something you saw or something from your imagination? Can you make up a story about your painting?
4. Watch the paper as it dries. The design will whiten and begin to crystallize.

Epsom-salt mixture

Try This!

Use wax crayons to draw a picture or design on dark paper (press heavily). Paint the Epsom-salt solution over the crayon design. As the solution dries, crystals will form on the paper wherever there is no crayon. This looks good with crayon drawings of winter scenes.

Invisible Drawing

Watch drawings appear before your eyes!

What You'll Need

candles (chunky white candles are easy to use)

paintbrush

plain art paper

watercolor paints

Books to Enjoy

The following books are illustrated beautifully with watercolor paints:

Old Turtle by Douglas Wood

Seashells by the Seashore by Marianne Berkes

Tuesday by David Weisner

What to Do

1. Use a candle to draw on a piece of art paper. Even though you cannot see your drawing now, you will later.

2. For this activity, the more wax the better, so press down hard. If little pieces of wax crumble and fall off, or if the candle breaks, don't worry.

3. Pick out two or three watercolors to paint on the paper, however you'd like. As you spread paint over the entire page, the secret designs and shapes you made with the candle will reveal themselves!

4. Hang your painting to dry.

white candle

watercolor

Try This!

Try the same activity on fabric instead of paper. Tape the fabric to a table. As you draw with the candle on fabric, press hard—harder than on paper.

Crayon Etchings

Scratch the surface, and create a classic etching.

What You'll Need

crayons, in many colors, including black

example of an etching from a book or from the Internet

paper clips

white or light paper

Books to Enjoy

Beady Bear by Don Freeman

Lunch by Denise Fleming

A Rainbow of My Own by Don Freeman

What to Do

1. Look at an example of a print.
2. Color a piece of paper with crayons, using any design. Use one color or many different colors.
3. Press hard as you color. Be sure to cover the entire surface of the paper.
4. When you are finished coloring your design on the paper, cover it completely with black crayon, again pressing very hard. What do you think the black layer is for?
5. Straighten a paper clip to form a point on one end. (You may need help from an adult to do this.)
6. Etch a design or picture in the black crayon using the paper clip. What are you drawing? Is it something real or something imagined? Did you know that the colors you used first would show through the black? What does this technique remind you of?

Try This!

Reverse the process: Fill the paper with black crayon first, and then cover the black crayon with colored crayons. Etch through the colored crayons to reveal the black crayon underneath.

CHAPTER 2

Drip, Drop, and Paint

Feather-Duster Painting

Bubbles, Bubbles, Bubbles

Rain Paintings

Ice Painting

Silly String Art

Painting with Magnets

Sprayed Leaves

Plastic-Wrap Painting

Soda-Straw Painting

Scratch-and-Sniff Painting

Drip Drip Dropper

Brush Away Art

Bubble Paint

Feather-Duster Painting

What does it look like when you paint with a feather duster instead of a paintbrush?
It's great when you paint something large and fluffy, like clouds.
But if you use an old duster, shake it out first!

What You'll Need

feather duster

large paper

liquid soap

liquid tempera paint

paint smock or old shirt

pie tins

Books to Enjoy

The Cloud Book
by Tomie dePaola

It Looks Like Spilt Milk
by Charles Shaw

What to Do

1. Pour tempera paint and a squirt of liquid soap into a pie tin. Swirl them together until the mixture is completely blended. (Use another tin and another feather duster for each color if you are painting with more than one color of paint.)
2. Dip a feather duster into the paint, and use the feather duster to create a design on a piece of paper.
3. Experiment with various techniques, such as dabbing, brushing, rolling, and slapping the feather duster on the paper. What designs can you create?
4. Try layering the colors, which produces a nice effect. Notice the colors and textures that appear.

smock

tempera paint and liquid soap

pie tin

Try This!

This painting technique is great for painting large objects, such as boxes, and for creating backgrounds for murals.

Rain Paintings

Rain may bring a rainbow, but did you know that rain can also make paintings? Next time it rains, try this technique.

What You'll Need

a gentle rain

large fingerpaint paper (coated paper is best for this activity)

large tray or cookie sheet

watercolor paint or liquid tempera paints

Books to Enjoy

In the Rain with Baby Duck by Amy Hest

Listen to the Rain by Bill Martin Jr. and John Archambault

One Hot Summer Day by Nina Crews

The Rainbabies by Laura Krauss Melmed

What to Do

1. Paint freely on a large sheet of fingerpaint paper.
2. Notice the colors in your painting. Continue until the entire paper is filled with paint.
3. When you finish painting, place the paper on a cookie sheet or tray.
4. Carry the cookie sheet or tray outside into the rain. Watch as the rain falls on your painting. What is happening when the raindrops hit the paper? Why is the paint splattering?
5. Watch the painting as it sits in the rain for a few minutes, then carry your artwork back inside, and allow it to dry.
6. After the painting has dried, describe how the rain affected your painting.

Try This!

Sprinkle dry tempera powder on the paper, and then place the paper on a tray or cookie sheet. Put the tray or cookie sheet outside in the rain, and leave it out until the paper is soaked through. Bring your artwork back inside, and let it dry. How is this painting different from the one you created with liquid paint?

Silly String Art

What can you create with a string that you cannot create with a paintbrush?

What You'll Need

construction paper

liquid tempera paint in a variety of colors

newspaper or old bedsheets

paint pans or pie tins

paint smock or old shirt

scissors

string or yarn

Books to Enjoy

The Big Ball of String by Ross Mueller

Cat's Cradle: A Book of String Figures by Anne A. Johnson

What to Do

1. Cover the area where you will work with newspaper or old sheets. Put on a paint smock or old shirt.
2. Pour tempera paint into paint pans or pie tins, one tin for each color of paint.
3. Cut string or yarn into 12" pieces. (You may need adult help with this step.)
4. Place a sheet of construction paper on the prepared area.
5. Hold one end of a piece of string, and dip the rest of it into the paint.
6. Take one paint-filled string and splat, whip, or twirl it onto the construction paper.
7. Experiment with different techniques, or combine different colors of paint.
8. Notice the colors and patterns in your string painting. What do you like about string painting? Why?

yarn

pie tin with paint

smock

old sheet

paper

Try This!

Create a story about what you see or imagine in the design of the paint.

Sprayed Leaves

This painting technique uses a stencil and creates something called a *silhouette*, which resembles the shadow of an object.

What You'll Need

easel

empty spray bottles, one for each color of paint

liquid tempera or watercolor paint

masking tape

newspaper

paper

scissors

stiff paper or acetate

Books to Enjoy

It's Fall! by Linda Glaser

Leaf Man by Lois Ehlert

What to Do

1. Cut out a large leaf shape from a piece of stiff paper or acetate. This will be the stencil. (You may need adult help with this step.)
   Hint: Save the leaf shape for another project. You will use the paper with the cut-out opening for this activity.

2. Attach paper to the easel, and then tape the leaf stencil on the paper. Make sure to put newspaper underneath the easel.

3. Choose a color of paint. Fill a spray bottle halfway with the paint.
   Hint: Add water so the paint is thin enough to spray out of the spray bottle.

4. Squirt paint over the leaf stencil. (You may need adult help and guidance to learn how to work the sprayer.)

5. Choose another color to spray on top of the first color, and repeat the process.

6. Remove the leaf stencil, and admire your leaf painting.

7. How do you like painting with a sprayer instead of a brush? Does the leaf you painted look like the leaves in your neighborhood? Which leaves do you like best? Why? Which fall leaf color is your favorite?

stencil easel paper newspaper spray bottles (2 colors)

Try This!

Create several leaf stencils of different shapes and sizes, and use several, one after the other, on the same sheet of paper, to make overlapping leaf patterns.

Soda-Straw Painting

If you can blow bubbles in your drink, you can make art, too!

What You'll Need

liquid tempera paint

masking tape

newspaper

paper

plastic soda straws

Books to Enjoy

The Dot by Peter H. Reynolds

I Ain't Gonna Paint No More!
by Karen Beaumont

Mouse Paint
by Ellen Stoll Walsh

What to Do

1. Cover the table with newspaper.
2. Tape a piece of paper onto the newspaper.
3. Scoop a spoonful of tempera paint, and place it on the paper, near the bottom.
4. Blow through the straw to move the paint without touching it. (You may need adult help or guidance to demonstrate how to create a design by moving the straw and changing the direction of the air.)

   Hint: Ask an adult to snip a small hole in the straw so you can't suck the paint into your mouth.
5. Your breath blowing through the straw is like the wind blowing outside. Can you blow softly like a spring breeze or harder like the wind in a rainstorm?
6. Compare the results of blowing with and without a straw. Which is easier? Which has better results? Why? (Channeling the air with a straw increases the pressure of the air, which provides better control.)
7. Name your creation. What does it look like? a spider? an octopus? a tree?

It looks like a frog!

small hole

tempera paint

Drip Drip Dropper

Did you ever wonder what would happen if clouds rained paint instead of water? Find out in this activity!

What You'll Need

eyedroppers

liquid tempera paint or watercolor paints, thinned with water

paint cups

paper or basket-style coffee filters

Books to Enjoy

Hattie and the Wild Waves by Barbara Cooney

The Painter by Peter Catalanotto

What to Do

1. Pour different colors of thin paint (tempera or watercolor paint with water added) into four or five paint cups, one color per cup.
2. Place an eyedropper into each cup, and then put the cups near the paper or coffee filter.
   Hint: Make sure the paper is absorbent; do not use fingerpaint paper or paper with a high gloss.
3. Enjoy using the eyedroppers to drip paint onto the paper. (You may need adult help and guidance to show you how to use an eyedropper: Place the dropper into the paint, squeeze the bulb at the top, release the bulb, pull the eyedropper out of the paint, and squeeze the dropper again to release the paint onto the paper or coffee filter.)
4. Notice how mixing two colors creates a third color.
5. What do you think of the patterns created by the colors "bleeding" into the paper and each other? Do the colors spread out in perfect circles? Does the paper absorb the paint quickly or slowly? What do you think would happen if raindrops had different colors?
6. Hang your masterpiece to dry.

Try This!

Cut out green strips of paper to represent flower stalks and leaves. Glue the flower stalks to a sheet of paper. Cut the paper or coffee filter in the shape of a flower. Paint the paper as described above. Add the painted flower to the flower stalk. You can even fold it or use multiple paper or filters to make a "fluffy flower." Glue the leaves to the flowers.

Bubble Paint

Who doesn't love bubbles? Use bubbles in a new way—to make art.

What You'll Need

liquid hand soap or
dish-washing liquid

liquid tempera paint (strong
colors such as blue, purple, or
red work best)

measuring cup

pan, 9" x 12"

straws

spoon

water

white paper

Books to Enjoy

Chavela and the Magic Bubble
by Monica Brown

The Wind Blew by Pat Hutchins

What to Do

1. Place the pan in a sink or outside on a warm, sunny day.
2. Fill the pan with water to about 1" from the top. Ask an adult if you need help.
3. Squeeze 4–8 ounces of liquid soap or dishwashing liquid into the pan.
4. Use the spoon to stir in about 1 cup of paint. Gently swirl the mixture together until it is well-blended.
5. Put one end of the straw into the mixture and blow gently. Experiment, and see what happens if you blow quickly versus slowly. The bubbles will rise above the top of the pan. Can you blow bubbles of different sizes?
6. Gently place a piece of paper on top of the bubbles. Carefully pick it up by holding the corners. Look at the patterns: Are all the bubbles the same, or are they different? Is the color dark or light?
7. Find an undisturbed spot for the bubble print to dry.

Try These Ideas!

- To make a great background for undersea pictures, use blue paint bubbles to make the water. Sponge-print fish onto the mural, and glue sand and shells on the bottom of the mural.
- When the first bubble print is dry, mix up another batch of bubble paint in a different color, and repeat the process using the same sheet of paper. What happens where the two colors blend?

Bubbles, Bubbles, Bubbles

Instead of wood-block prints, make bubble-pop prints!

What You'll Need

bubble wand

cup

food coloring or liquid watercolor paint

liquid dishwashing soap

old shower curtain

scissors

water

white construction paper

Book to Enjoy

Bubble Trouble
by Margaret Mahy

What to Do

1. Before starting, cover a table or the floor with an old shower curtain.
2. Place a piece of construction paper on the shower curtain.
3. Fill your cup about one-quarter full with water.
4. Add a small amount of liquid dishwashing soap and one color of food coloring or liquid watercolor paint to the cup. Use a bubble wand to gently stir the mixture.
5. Dip the bubble wand in the colored water, and then blow bubbles onto the construction paper. The bubbles will land on the paper and make bubble prints.
6. Practice blowing bubbles different ways: large bubbles and small bubbles, a fast stream of bubbles and a slow procession of bubbles.
7. Look at the various bubble prints you created. How are they alike and different? Which one is your favorite?
8. If you want to, get another sheet of construction paper, and try to cover it with only your favorite kind of bubbles.

Try This!

Prepare cups of different colored bubble mixtures, and create multicolored prints.

old shower curtain

white construction paper

bubble-pop print

25

Ice Painting

Melting ice may be messy, but it can create pretty pictures.

What You'll Need

dry tempera paint

ice cubes, ice chips

newspaper or an old shower curtain

paint smock or old shirt

plain paper

plastic spoons

small, shallow cups

Books to Enjoy

Art & Max by David Wiesner

Growing Colors by Bruce McMillan

What to Do

1. Put on a paint smock or old shirt. You might also want to cover your art area with newspaper or an old shower curtain.
2. Use a spoon to scoop dry tempera paint into shallow cups, one color per cup.
3. Sprinkle the dry powder onto your paper in small quantities with a spoon.
4. After sprinkling the powder on your paper, scatter a few ice chips around the paper. Find a sunny window or spot on the floor, and carefully move the paper to that spot. What do you think will happen next?
5. After a few minutes, check the melting ice chips and see what happens when they mix with the paint powder. Is that the effect you predicted?

plastic spoon

smock

tempera paints

plain paper

ice chips

dry tempera paint

old shower curtain

Painting with Magnets

Find some metal objects—not too heavy but not too light—
and watch them magically move paint around your paper.

What You'll Need

box

liquid tempera or watercolor
paint

magnets

metal object, such as a paper
clip or a washer

paper

small bowl

spoon or eyedropper

Books to Enjoy

*Magnets: Pulling Together, Pushing
Apart* by Natalie Rosinsky

What Makes a Magnet?
by Franklyn Branley

What to Do

1. Place the paper in the box.
2. Pour some paint into a bowl. Gradually add water to the paint to thin it out. Using a spoon or an eyedropper, scatter a few drops of thinned paint around the paper. (You may need adult help and guidance to show you how to use an eyedropper: Place the dropper into the paint, squeeze the bulb at the top, release the bulb, pull the eyedropper out of the paint, and squeeze the dropper again to release the paint onto the paper.)
3. Place a metal object on the paper. Hold the magnet underneath the box where it will attract the metal object, then move the magnet around, pulling the metal object across the paper.
4. As the metal object moves with the magnet, the paint gets dragged around and makes designs. What happens if you move the magnet quickly? slowly? If you break the contact between the magnet and the metal object and then place the magnet under the box and near the metal object on the paper, what happens? Does the metal object slide over to the magnet? Is it able to push the paint around when it does that? What effect does that create?

holding the
magnet
underneath

paint   washer

27

Plastic-Wrap Painting

Putting plastic wrap over paint is a very cool way
to create a painting!

What You'll Need

liquid tempera paint

paper

plastic wrap

spoons

Books to Enjoy

Little Blue and Little Yellow
by Leo Lionni

Mouse Paint
by Ellen Stoll Walsh

Who Said Red?
by Mary Serfozo

What to Do

1. Use a spoon to put two or three colors of paint onto your paper.
2. Ask an adult to help you cut a piece of plastic wrap slightly larger than the paper. If it clings to itself, gently pull the plastic wrap apart.
3. Lay the piece of plastic wrap over the paint and paper.
4. Gently rub and twist the wrap with your fingertips. Squish the colors together, creating interesting shapes. Smooth the paint around. What does it feel like? What does the paint do when you push on the wrap? What happens when the colors blend?
5. Find a safe place to store the painting while it dries with the plastic wrap on it. The plastic wrap will stick to the paint, creating an interesting effect.

Try This!

After you squish the paint around the paper, write alphabet letters and numbers with your fingers.

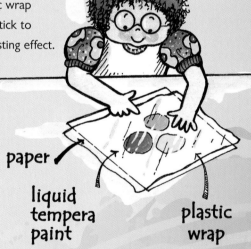

paper

liquid
tempera
paint

plastic
wrap

Scratch-and-Sniff Painting

Art never smelled so good!

What You'll Need

measuring spoons

newspaper

packets of unsweetened drink mix in a variety of flavors

paintbrushes

small bowls

spoons for mixing

water

white or light-colored paper, 8" x 10"

Books to Enjoy

Eat the Fruit, Plant the Seed
by Millicent E. Selsam

From Seed to Pear
by Ali Mitgutsch

What to Do

1. Cover the work area with newspapers.
2. Prepare the "paint" by mixing 1 tablespoon water with each packet of drink mix in separate bowls, one color per bowl.
3. Paint with the drink mixes just as you would with any other kind of paint. How is the drink-mix solution different from regular paint? Is it thicker or thinner? Are the colors bright or soft?
4. Choose a safe spot where your painting can dry.
5. After the painting dries, scratch the painting with your fingernail. What happens? Do the different colors have different scents? Can you identify the smells?
6. Mix the paints on the paper to get a whole new scent! Experiment, and have fun!

paints

Ummmm

newspapers

29

Brush Away Art

Use everyday objects (after getting permission, of course!) to create all kinds of interesting textures and effects.

What You'll Need

different kinds of brushes, such as hair, dog, tooth, basting, vegetable, clothing, scrub, and paintbrushes in varied widths

---

liquid tempera paint in assorted colors

---

mural paper, 3' x 6'

---

newspaper

Styrofoam or aluminum trays

Books to Enjoy

The Legend of the Indian Paintbrush retold by Tomie dePaola

Stephanie's Ponytail by Robert Munsch

What to Do

1. Cover the floor with newspaper. Next, put mural paper on top of the newspaper.
2. Carefully pour the paint into trays.
3. Paint a mural using a variety of brushes—you can create a scene from a story, something out of your imagination, or whatever you like!
4. Experiment with several brushes and colors, noting the differences in the appearance of the paint. What effects are created by the different brushes? Do the results look like you thought they would? If not, what did you think they would look like? What is each brush used for?

mural paper

tooth brush

clothing brush

dog brush

wallpaper brush

basting brush

Sandy and Sticky

Just Beachy!

Have a beach vacation anytime by creating your very own seashore!

What You'll Need

blue food coloring

dried seaweed or sea kelp
(real if possible; if not,
you can make these out of
crepe paper)

garden hose and outside faucet

playdough or clay that will
harden in air

sand and sandbox

sand molds

sand pails and shovels

seashells

spray bottle and water

Books to Enjoy

At the Beach by Anne Rockwell
and Harlow Rockwell

A Beach for the Birds
by Bruce McMillan

The Castle Builder
by Dennis Nolan

What to Do

1. Think about what a beach looks like. If you are not sure, look at a book about the beach. If your family has been to the beach, what do you remember? Mark off areas of your sandbox to represent the various aspects of a real beach. For example, mark the dunes, the high-tide mark, and the surf.

2. Use a stick to mark a line in the sand that shows where the sand and ocean water meet on the beach. This is called the *shoreline*.

3. Fill the spray bottle with water, and mix in blue food coloring to create a bright blue. (If you need help, ask an adult for guidance.) Spray the "ocean" part of your sandbox bright blue. If you need help working the sprayer at first, ask an adult to show you how or to help you squeeze.

4. When you finish making the "water," spread seashells and sea kelp or seaweed over the "beach" area.

5. You also can use a shovel and pail to move the sand around to form sand dunes, and use the sand molds to make sand castles. Think about the different kinds of life found in the ocean and on the beach.

6. If you want to, add ocean creatures. Mold fish, octopi, sea lions, oysters, snails, and other sea-dwelling creatures from clay or playdough. Place your creations on the "beach" or in the "water" where they will air-dry quickly.

7. Stand back and enjoy your huge work of art!

Try This!

Add more details, such as paper "beach towels," clay or playdough people, or paper umbrellas, to your beach scene.

Sandpaper Art

Coloring on sandpaper? The end result may surprise you!

What You'll Need

cookie sheet

crayons

oven mitts

oven or toaster oven

sandpaper

timer

Book to Enjoy

The Art Lesson by Tomie dePaola

What to Do

1. Draw a picture or symbols using crayons on a piece of sandpaper (which can be a regular sheet or cut into your favorite shape)—press hard! What did you draw, and why?

2. Place the drawing on a cookie sheet. You will need an adult to help you weigh down the edges with heavy, ovenproof items so the sandpaper will not curl from the heat. Ask an adult to heat the oven to 350°F and then put the cookie sheet in the oven.

3. Set the timer for 20 minutes. As the sandpaper heats, think about what is going to happen to your artwork.

4. When the timer goes off, ask an adult to remove the cookie sheet from the oven.

5. After your sandpaper picture cools, look at the changes in your picture. Are the changes what you expected?

6. Cut a frame out of construction paper for your shiny work of art!

Try This!

After the pictures are removed from the oven, ask an adult to place your Sandpaper Art on a large cutting board. Immediately place a white piece of paper over the top of the Sandpaper Art and rub the white paper with your hand. The melted crayon will rub off onto the paper, making a print.

Sand Art

Create miniature sandscapes, or store colored sand for future art.

What You'll Need

bowls

clear glass saltshakers

food coloring

funnel

glue

paper

sand

spoon, fork, or other stirring utensil

spray bottle with water

Books to Enjoy

The Art Lesson
by Tomie dePaola

Little Blue and Little Yellow
by Leo Lionni

What to Do

1. Pour sand in several bowls (use as many bowls as you have colors).
2. Use the spray bottle to spray the sand until it is slightly damp. If necessary, ask an adult for guidance or hand-over-hand support to help you squeeze.
3. Drop one color of food coloring into each bowl of sand.
4. Using a spoon, fork, or other stirring utensil, mix the food coloring thoroughly with the sand. Stir the color so that it spreads evenly throughout the sand.
5. Move the sand to an undisturbed spot so it can dry. Sun or a low-temperature oven will speed up the drying process.
6. After the sand dries, pour sand through the funnel into the saltshakers. Ask an adult for help if you need to.

Try This!

Dribble a design on paper using glue, then shake colored sand on top to create a sand painting. Let the glue dry, then gently shake the excess sand off.

saltshaker

colored sand

glue

34

Seashore Pictures

Even if you don't live by the shore, you can still have an ocean view!

What You'll Need

aluminum foil

blue marker or paint

glue

paintbrushes, two, medium size

plastic wrap

poster board

sand

seashells, various types

small stones

tape

Books to Enjoy

A Beach Day by Douglas Florian

The Seashore Book by Charlotte Zolotow

Those Summers by Aliki

What to Do

1. Brush or spread a thin layer of glue on the bottom third of a piece of poster board.
2. Sprinkle or drizzle sand onto the glue to create a beach. If the sand piles up, don't worry! Hold the sides of the paper, and gently shake off the excess.
3. Dip the shells into glue, and attach them to the poster board on top of the sand.
4. Use glue to add pebbles or small stones.
5. Crumple up a piece of aluminum foil, and then uncrumple it. (Don't try to smooth out the wrinkles!) Glue it flat onto the paper above the sand.
6. Color the foil with a blue marker or paint to make the water.
7. Put plastic wrap over the blue-colored foil to give the effect of water. If you need to, ask an adult to hold the plastic wrap around the edges of the paper so you can tape the edges down.

Try These Ideas!

- Make up an original story to go with the beach picture, and you or an adult can write it down. Or, the two of you can work together to tell a story by taking turns describing and talking about the items in your picture.
- Count the number of shells and rocks used in the picture. How do shells and rocks look the same and different from each other?
- Find a book about shells, and look through it to identify the shells in your picture.

Spiderweb Designs

Different spiders weave different patterns in their webs.
What kinds of patterns can you make?

What You'll Need

black paint

glitter glue (optional)

glue

markers

plastic paper-plate holder
(the kind with
weblike designs on it)

scissors

sponges

white and black paper

Books to Enjoy

The Itsy Bitsy Spider
by Iza Trapani

The Very Busy Spider
by Eric Carle

What to Do

1. Flip the plate holder over so that the bottom faces up.
2. Cover the bottom of the holder with black paint by dabbing or brushing paint on with sponges.
3. Flip the plate holder back over, then press the paint-covered bottom onto a piece of white paper. When you lift the holder, you should discover a weblike print.
4. If needed, ask an adult to help you cut out circles and thin strips of black construction paper. Create spiders out of the black circles and strips. Think about spiders and what they do to help people (they eat bugs). What does a web look like after it rains or in the morning dew? How many kinds of spiders are there? Decorate your spiders and spider-webs with paint or glitter glue.
5. Glue the spiders onto their "webs."

glue to design

spider

glitter

white paper

web

black paint

Try These Ideas!

- Make more than one web print on a piece of paper, overlapping the designs.
- Use a variety of paint colors instead of just black.
- Use berry baskets to make prints. Just dip them into paint and print! After making berry-basket prints, eat the berries that came in the baskets, and read *Jamberry* by Bruce Degen.

Glue Webs

Spin your own web of glue and glitter,
then hang your creation from the ceiling with string.

What You'll Need

glitter or food coloring
(optional)

glue, in squeeze bottles

string

wax paper

Books to Enjoy

Aaaarrgghh! Spider!
by Lydia Monks

*Anansi the Spider: A Tale from the
Ashanti* by Gerald McDermott

What to Do

1. Get a large piece of wax paper. If you need help, ask an adult to help you tear a sheet from the box.

2. Squeeze glue all over the wax paper to make a web design. This project works best if you use thick lines of glue and leave a few spaces in the middle of the glue globs. Look at your lines and swirls, and notice whether they are thick or thin, straight or curvy. How are they similar? How are they different?

   Hint: Add glitter or food coloring to the glue before you squeeze it onto wax paper. You could use commercial glitter glue and eliminate this step.

3. Pick a safe spot to keep the wax paper while the glue dries. Allow the glue to dry completely.

4. With an adult's help, slowly peel the wax paper away from the dried glue.

5. Hang your web from the ceiling with string.

glitter

Glowing Globes of Glue

Make an Earth suncatcher!

What You'll Need

blue food coloring

brown and green permanent markers

cup

glue

margarine-tub lid

permanent markers

pictures of Earth from space (from a book, magazine, or the Internet)

spoon

yarn or string

Books to Enjoy

The Earth Book by Todd Parr

On Earth by G. Brian Karas

What to Do

1. Squeeze glue into a cup, filling the cup about one-third full. Squirt 5–8 drops of blue food coloring into the glue, then use a spoon to mix the color into the glue.

2. Pour some of the glue into a margarine-tub lid (Don't fill it to the brim!). Find a safe spot where the glue can dry undisturbed in the margarine-tub lid, and let it dry completely. This may take several days, depending upon the humidity.
   Hint: Store any remaining glue in an airtight container.

3. When the glue is completely dry, peel the blue circle formed by the dry glue away from the lid.

4. Notice that you can see light through the blue circle of dried glue.

5. Ask an adult to show you pictures of Earth taken from space, so you can see what land and clouds look like from above. Notice all the blue, which is water.

6. Carefully draw landforms on the blue circle (with permanent markers). Use one color for mountains and another for flat lands.

7. Your Earth glue globe should stick to a glass window. If it doesn't, ask an adult to punch a hole in the top, and thread a piece of yarn or ribbon through it to hang the Earth globe in a window.

Try This!

Use different shades of food coloring to make a variety of glue globes.

flat lands

mountains

Drizzle Goo

Turn out tactile art, and explore the textures
and patterns of everyday objects.

What You'll Need

1 cup flour

¼ cup salt

¼ cup sugar

¾ cup water (more for a
thinner consistency)

food coloring

measuring cups and spoons

mixing bowls and spoons

paper

paper products such as egg
cartons, paper tubes, paper
towels, and paper plates

squeeze bottles such as
detergent or shampoo
containers

Book to Enjoy

I Can Tell by Touching
by Carolyn Otto

What to Do

1. Combine 1 cup flour, ¼ cup salt, ¼ cup sugar, and ¾ cup water in a mixing bowl, stirring well.

2. Divide the mixture into portions. Add a few drops of food coloring to each portion until you get the brightness or shade of color you want.

3. Pour each portion of the mixture into a clean, empty squeeze bottle, one color per bottle.

4. Drizzle the goo onto paper and other surfaces, such as egg cartons, paper tubes, paper towels, or paper plates. Make interesting shapes and designs.

5. Let the goo harden in an out-of-the-way place until it dries thoroughly. This may take a day or more. The goo will keep its shape unless the mixture is too thin.

6. After the goo has hardened, close your eyes and feel the shapes or designs with your fingers. What do the shapes feel like? How do the different paper backgrounds change the way the shapes and designs feel?

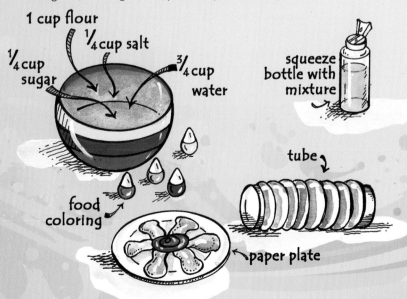

1 cup flour
¼ cup salt
¼ cup sugar
¾ cup water
food coloring
squeeze bottle with mixture
tube
paper plate

39

Nuts About Nature

Grass Haircut

Plant several cups of grass, and style each face's "hair" in a different way. Try a buzz cut, long hair, a ponytail, or braids.

What You'll Need

black marker

children's safety scissors

grass seeds

large Styrofoam cup

potting soil

small watering can

trowel or large spoon

water

Books to Enjoy

The Carrot Seed by Ruth Krauss

The Hair of Zoe Fleefenbacher Goes to School by Laurie Halse Anderson

Hats Off to Hair! by Virginia Kroll

How a Seed Grows by Helene J. Jordan

In the Tall, Tall Grass by Denise Fleming

What to Do

1. Draw eyes, a nose, and a mouth on the outside of the cup.
2. Add potting soil to the cup, about two-thirds full.
3. Sprinkle grass seeds on top of the soil, then cover the seeds with a small amount of soil.
4. When you finish covering the seeds, pour a small amount of water into the cup. What do you think will happen? Do you think the grass will grow quickly or slowly? Why do you think you drew a face on the cup? How tall do you think the grass can grow?
5. After several days, when the grass grows and reaches a height of 1" to 2" above the rim of the cup, trim the grass with safety scissors. If you need help working the scissors, ask an adult how to use the scissors or ask him to put his hands over yours and guide you.

Try These Ideas!

- Pull up a few of the blades of grass as they grow, and examine the roots.
- Cut out butterflies and bugs from construction paper, and use them to decorate the grass.

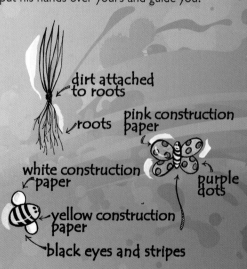

1" cut off the top

grass

dirt

paper cup with face

grass seeds

dirt

watering can

dirt attached to roots

roots

pink construction paper

purple dots

white construction paper

yellow construction paper

black eyes and stripes

Build a Nest

Create a snug, safe nest, just like birds do. Determine which materials work best, and then use these materials to make your nest.

What You'll Need

found items, such as bits of fabric, thread, and grass; craft feathers; dryer lint; pine needles or regular straw; and twigs, broken into very small pieces

homemade glue (recipe below)

large mixing bowl

petroleum jelly

Recipe for Glue

½ teaspoon alum (available in the spice section of grocery stores)

¼ cup flour

¼ cup sugar

1¾ cups water, divided

Mix the sugar, flour, and alum in a pan. Gradually add 1 cup water, and stir briskly. Heat to boiling, and boil until the mixture is clear and smooth. Add ¾ cup water, and stir. (Double or triple this recipe as needed, according to the size of your nest. This recipe is for a small nest.)

What to Do

1. Collect the items you plan to use to make the nest. Make the glue using the recipe below, with an adult's help.
2. Smear the petroleum jelly inside the mixing bowl using your hands or a paper towel.
3. Ask an adult to help you apply a thin layer of the glue mixture. (Paintbrushes might help.)
4. Dump the found items out on a table. Sort out the lint and feathers, and set them aside to be used last.
5. Add the other found items to the mixing bowl, pressing them firmly against the glue mixture. After you have covered the glue with material, apply another layer of glue. Cover that layer with more nest materials, always pressing them firmly. Keep the shape as round as possible, and remember to fill in the bottom.
6. Work until you use up all the materials and glue.
7. Add the feathers and lint to line the nest, just as a real bird would.
8. Carefully move the nest to a warm place where it can dry for several hours.
9. After the glue has dried, gently remove the nest from the mixing bowl. It will probably still be a little moist and messy. Place it on a sturdy surface where you can leave it.
10. Push down on the bottom to flatten it slightly, and lift up on the edges to form a nice, round shape. The nest will continue to dry over the next couple of days.

Feathered Friends

Make a flock of birds to fly across your ceiling.

What You'll Need

construction paper

craft feathers

crayons or markers (optional)

glue

medium-sized googly eyes (optional)

scissors

Books to Enjoy

Are You My Mother? by P. D. Eastman

The Best Nest by P. D. Eastman

A Nest Full of Eggs by Priscilla Belz Jenkins

What to Do

1. Cut out a bird shape from construction paper. (If you need help, ask an adult to trace a bird shape for you.)
2. Spread the glue onto the paper where you want to put feathers.
3. Place the craft feathers on top of the glue.
4. Put glue onto the back of googly eyes, and place the eyes on the bird's head. Or you can use crayons or markers to draw eyes on the bird's head.
5. Let the bird dry completely.
6. You can hang your bird from the ceiling with yarn. If you plan to hang your creation, remember to decorate both sides of the bird.

Try These Ideas!

- Go for a walk, and look for birds that live in your neighborhood.
- Use other materials to decorate your bird. Two suggestions are sequins or bits of colorful fabric.

Bird pattern

hole for string

googly eye

decorate on both sides

Fall Wreath

Celebrate the season with a pretty, natural wreath.

What You'll Need

cardboard, poster board, or heavy card stock

found natural materials that are plentiful in autumn, such as dried leaves, milkweed pods and seeds, acorns, pressed flowers, wheat stalks

glue

hole punch

red or orange watercolor paints or crayons

red yarn

Books to Enjoy

Chicken Soup with Rice
by Maurice Sendak

Leaf Trouble
by Jonathan Emmett

Red Leaf, Yellow Leaf
by Lois Ehlert

What to Do

1. Go on a nature walk, and collect natural items that are plentiful in the fall, such as dried leaves, milkweed pods and seeds, acorns, flowers, wheat stalks, and so forth. (For flowers, carefully press them between sheets of paper, and dry them in a heavy book for a couple of days.)

2. Cut a wreath shape out of cardboard, poster board, or heavy paper. Ask an adult for help or guidance, if necessary. Use the hole punch to make a hole at the top of the wreath.

3. Paint or color the wreath shape however you would like. Think about the colors you see a lot of during fall. Which color is your favorite? least favorite? Why? Think about what you saw and picked up on your nature walk.

4. Let the wreath dry undisturbed.

5. While the paint on the wreath is drying, spread the natural items out on a table. Sort through them, and pick out ones you like for your wreath. Arrange them however you would like.

6. Glue the natural items onto the wreath. When the glue is dry, thread yarn through the hole to make a loop, and tie the yarn in a knot. If you need help with this step, ask an adult. Voilà! Your wreath is ready for hanging!

Try This!

Make other seasonal wreaths. For spring, make heart-shaped wreaths, and use paper doilies and dried flowers tied with pink ribbons. For summer, make a beach wreath using dribbled sand, shells, bay leaves, pebbles, and so forth. For winter, use cones from different evergreens (especially little hemlock cones), whole cinnamon sticks, star-shaped anise, nuts, and red ribbon.

Hint: If you are using heavy materials to decorate your wreath, be sure to use cardboard for the base.

Leaf Bookmarks

Preserve interesting leaves as bookmarks, and give your creations as gifts.

What You'll Need

clear contact paper

glue, in a squeeze bottle

hole punch

leaves, ferns, and grasses

thin paintbrushes

thread or yarn

watercolor paints

watercolor paper cut into rectangular bookmark shapes

Books to Enjoy

Autumn: An Alphabet Acrostic by Steven Schnur

Chicka Chicka Boom Boom by Bill Martin, Jr. and John Archambault

Red Leaf, Yellow Leaf by Lois Ehlert

The Seasons of Arnold's Apple Tree by Gail Gibbons

What to Do

1. Go on a walk, and collect small leaves, ferns, and grasses. Examine what they look like, and see how many different kinds you can find. Which ones are your favorites?
2. Lay them on newspaper, or press them between the pages of books until the leaves or grasses are dry. This may take a few days.
3. While waiting for the plant bits to dry, paint the bookmark shapes. You can paint them all one color, in patterns, or use several colors per bookmark—whatever strikes your fancy!
4. Let the bookmarks dry.
5. Set out the dried, pressed plants, and glue them on the bookmarks in arrangements of your choice.
6. Ask an adult to help you cover the bookmarks with clear contact paper. Smooth out the contact paper, and get rid of any lines, bubbles, or bumps.
7. Use the hole punch to make a hole at the top of each bookmark. If necessary, ask an adult to put her hand over yours to help squeeze the hole punch with enough force.
8. Loop yarn or thread through the hole, and tie it in a knot to make a tassel.

①rectangle shape

②paint bookmark

③glue dried, pressed plants on bookmark

④cover bookmark with clear contact paper

⑤punch hole

Nature Note Cards

Make personal stationery with flowers you find and dry yourself.

What You'll Need

clean newsprint
(from an art store)

collecting basket or box

drying table or floor area

heavy books

plain note cards

white glue in squeeze bottle

Books to Enjoy

Chrysanthemum
by Kevin Henkes

The Empty Pot by Demi

Planting a Rainbow by Lois Ehlert

Plants That Never Ever Bloom
by Ruth Heller

This Year's Garden
by Cynthia Rylant

What to Do

1. Go on a walk, and collect a variety of blossoms in a basket or box. Try to identify the blossoms as you collect them. (Ask an adult, or look in a flower book, if you need help.) How are they alike and different? Which flower is your favorite?

2. Find a drying area that can be left undisturbed for several days. This could be a table or a corner of the floor. Once you find a spot, spread out several sheets of clean newsprint.

3. Remove the flowers from your collection box, and arrange them on the newsprint. The blossoms should not touch each other as they dry.

4. Cover the flowers with another sheet of clean newsprint, and put some heavy books on top. (Ask an adult for help.) Leave the blossoms undisturbed for three days.

5. After the third day, remove the books and the top layer of newsprint. Slowly and carefully peel away any blossoms stuck to the newsprint.

6. Create interesting arrangements with the dried blossoms on plain note cards. Arrange them by color, size, type, or in any way that suits your fancy. You could also choose to put just one blossom on each card.

7. Glue the blossoms onto the note cards by painting glue on the bottom of each blossom and then placing the blossom or blossoms on the card. If the blossoms are small or fragile, water down the glue, and paint this thinned glue over the blossom. Allow to dry overnight.

Try This!

Use the dried blossoms or leaves to create flower pictures that you frame.

Berry Purple Paint

Did you ever wonder how people long ago made inks, dyes, and paints?
Make your own natural dyes, and see if you get the colors you expect.

What You'll Need

3 bowls

brown onion skins

fork or tongs

glue and paper

juice from 1 can of beets

juice from 1 can of blueberries

newsprint or plastic

paintbrush

pan of water

stove

white cotton or flannel, cut
into three strips about 1" x 5"

Books to Enjoy

Charlie Needs a Cloak
by Tomie dePaola

*The Legend of the Indian
Paintbrush* by Tomie dePaola

Pelle's New Suit by Elsa Beskow

What to Do

1. Ask an adult to place the onion skins in a pan, cover them with water, and bring the mixture to a boil on the stove. Look at the liquid from time to time. How does it change? What does it smell like? Boil until it creates a brown liquid. Ask an adult to turn off the heat and move the pan from the heat. After the mixture cools, use a fork or tongs to remove the onion skins from the water, and discard them.

2. Carefully pour the beet juice into one bowl and the blueberry juice into another bowl. Then pour the onion-skin liquid into a third bowl.

3. Carry each bowl to the table. Look at the foods they came from. What colors are the foods? What colors are the liquids in the bowls?

4. Dip a strip of cloth into the beet juice, remove it, and squeeze it out. What color is the strip?

5. Do the same with two more pieces of cloth, one for the blueberry juice and one for the onion-skin juice. Look at the colors. Are they what you expected?

6. Spread the strips out on newsprint or plastic to dry.

7. When the strips are dry, glue them to paper to create a collage, or use a paintbrush and the dye to "paint" a picture.

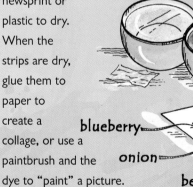

onion skin   blueberry   beet

blueberry

onion

beet

Blooming Tablecloth

What You'll Need

collection of fresh flowers, blossoms, buds, and leaves

flat, hard work surface such as a concrete floor

paper grocery bags, cut open and flattened out

permanent marker (optional)

plain white tablecloth or sheet

hammer and table knife

Books to Enjoy

The Flower Alphabet Book by Jerry Pallotta

Flower Garden by Eve Bunting and Kathryn Hewitt

Hint: To launder the tablecloth, ask an adult to wash it in cold water only. Add a cup of vinegar to the water to set the dye. Even so, expect the colors to fade significantly. Do not use bleach; dry the tablecloth on low.

What to Do

1. Before starting, spread the grocery bags out on a concrete floor or other hard work surface. Choose a surface that can take pounding with a hammer.

2. Spread half of the tablecloth out over the grocery bags. Let the other half spread out on the floor for now.

3. Arrange the blossoms and leaves over the part of the tablecloth on the grocery bags. Group and arrange blossoms and leaves by color, type, size, in a pattern, or any other grouping.

4. Fold the other half of the tablecloth gently and carefully over the arrangement so the blossoms don't blow away. You may need an adult to help you with this.

5. Next, feel with your fingers where the covered blossoms are. When you find the flowers and leaves, pound on them with the hammer until the juices and colors soak through the fabric. Be careful not to pound so long and hard that you make a hole in the fabric. **Caution:** This step must be carefully supervised by an adult.

6. Move on to other blossoms and leaves, continuing to hammer until all the blossoms have been pounded and their colors have soaked into the tablecloth.

7. Take one corner of the tablecloth, and ask an adult to pick up the other corner of the tablecloth. Together, unfold the tablecloth.

8. Carefully scrape off the plant bits and pieces with a table knife, and brush extra bits away with the palm of your hand. (You may need adult help with this step.)

9. Take the tablecloth inside, and use it to cover a table, showing the naturally colored fabric.

10. To complement the tablecloth, fill a vase with the same kinds of flowers, and place it in the center of the table.

Try This!

Create napkins or a table runner using the same directions.

Pressed-Flower Place Mats

What You'll Need

fresh flowers such as buttercups, violets, mock orange blossoms, pansies, or any flower with delicate petals

iron

newspapers

old telephone books or other heavy books

paper napkins

wax paper

Books to Enjoy

The Empty Pot by Demi

The Gardener by Sarah Stewart

What to Do

1. Ahead of time, ask an adult to help you tear wax paper in sheets approximately 28" long. Fold the wax paper sheets in half.
2. Take a walk to collect fresh flowers, or purchase flowers from elsewhere.
3. Open a paper napkin halfway, and place a flower facedown on it (make sure the petals spread out!), then close the napkin again. Repeat with more flowers and napkins.
4. Carefully place the napkins inside a telephone book or some other large, heavy book.
5. When you have put all the blossoms in napkins and in the phone books, stack extra weight on top of the telephone books. Set the books in a safe place where they won't be disturbed for about a week, leaving the flowers to dry.
6. Once the flowers have dried, ask an adult to preheat the iron to medium, no steam. (Ironing is an adult-only step.)
7. Carefully remove the dried flowers from the telephone books. Open the napkins so you can see the dried blossoms. Do they look different from the last time you saw them?
8. Place a sheet of folded wax paper on a pad of newspapers, and open it. Gently arrange several of the dried flowers on the wax paper, then fold the wax paper again, covering them. Cover with more newspapers or an old towel.
9. Ask an adult to press the wax paper with the iron to fuse the two sheets of wax paper. Repeat the process with the remaining flowers and additional sheets of wax paper.
10. Trim the finished product to the desired size.

Try These Ideas!

- Trim the wax paper to make bookmarks.
- Trim the finished product to fit inside a clear plastic lid; affix with double-sided tape, and punch a hole in the lid to make a suncatcher. Wrap in handmade paper for Mother's Day or another special occasion. In the fall, follow the same steps using leaves.

Nature Brushes

What You'll Need

craft feathers

pine needles

sticks

tempera or watercolor paint

water

white paper

Books to Enjoy

Earth Mother by Ellen Jackson

Earthdance by Joanne Ryder

From Pinecone to Pine Tree by Ellen Weiss

From Seed to Plant by Gail Gibbons

To Every Thing There Is a Season by Leo and Diane Dillon

What to Do

1. Sort through the feathers, pine needles, leaves, and sticks. What kind of effect do you think each item will create when you use it as a paintbrush?
2. Get some paper and some watercolor paints, and get to work! Use as many of the items as possible. Which effect do you like best? Why?
3. Find a safe spot for your painting to dry.

feather art

needle art

tempera paints

feathers

stick art

white paper

pine needles

Create with Color

Magic Dough

Why settle for ordinary playdough
when you can make dough that magically changes colors?

What You'll Need

food coloring

place mat or table covering to
protect table

plain playdough (Use the
recipe on this page or your
favorite.)

tray

Books to Enjoy

Clay Boy by Mirra Ginsburg

Create Anything with Clay
by Sherri Haab and
Laura Torres (eds.)

What to Do

❶ Before you start, ask an adult to prepare plain playdough from the recipe on this page or any other recipe. Help as much as you can.

❷ Form playdough into balls, about 2" in diameter.

❸ Poke a finger into one of the balls of dough. Drop in a small dot of food coloring. Close the color over with playdough. Poke another hole, and add another tiny drop of color, then close the hole. Make a third hole for a third color. Do this for all of the balls of dough, some with two holes, some with three.

❹ Explore, roll, manipulate, and squeeze the balls of playdough. As you play with the dough, the colors will start to mix into rainbow colors, eventually completely changing the color of the ball of dough.

Hint: Consider wearing latex gloves and an old shirt to protect your hands and clothes.

Playdough Recipe

2 cups flour
3 tablespoons oil
1 cup salt
2 cups boiling water
mixing bowl and spoon

Mix the dry ingredients in a bowl. Ask an adult to add the boiling water and oil. When the mixture is cool enough to handle, knead it into a workable dough, adding more flour, if necessary.

Try This!

Use your colorful dough to make sculptures.

Mosaic Flowers

Create a mosaic design by using small pieces of colored materials to form a picture.

What You'll Need

cup

glue

markers

old magazines

old paintbrushes

poster board cut into
a 6" square

scissors

water

Books to Enjoy

Alison's Zinnia by Anita Lobel

Colors Everywhere
by Tana Hoban

Mosaic Zoo
by Barbara Benson Keith

What to Do

1. Choose a color or many colors for the mosaic flower you want to create.
2. Look through the magazines for pictures with shades of that color. When you find the pictures you want, cut them out, and then cut the pictures into small squares. (Ask an adult for help, if you need it.)
3. Squeeze glue into a cup, then add some water to the glue. Mix together well. Spread a coat of glue on the poster board with a paintbrush.
4. Arrange your color squares on the poster board so they overlap and cover the entire board.
5. Let the poster board dry completely.
6. Turn the poster board over. Draw or trace a flower pattern on the reverse side.
7. Cut out the flower pattern.
8. Turn the poster board back over, and spread a thin coat of glue over the top of the colored squares.
9. Let your Mosaic Flower dry.

— Front —
6" square
different colors
cover entire area

— Back —
turn over
draw design and cut out

Try These Ideas!

- Create Mosaic Flower jewelry pins by cutting out several smaller flowers and gluing or taping safety pins to the backs of the flowers. Give the pins as a gifts.
- Attach a pipe cleaner stem and paper leaves to the flower.

55

Tissue-Transfer Rainbow Designs

Capture the hazy colors of rainbows using tissue paper.

What You'll Need

strips of brightly colored tissue paper (at least three colors)

water

white drawing or construction paper

wide paintbrushes

Books to Enjoy

The Alaska Mother Goose by Shelley Gill

All the Colors of the Rainbow by Allan Fowler

Elmer and the Rainbow by David McKee

Northern Lights: A Hanukkah Story by Diana Cohen Conway

White Rabbit's Color Book by Alan Baker

What to Do

❶ Using water and paintbrushes, wet down your paper.

❷ Lay the strips of tissue across the wet paper. Arrange the strips in a pattern of your choosing. Think about rainbows: Have you seen one? What did it look like? Were the colors bright or muted? Was it big or small? What colors were in the rainbow? How is a rainbow made?

❸ Overlap the tissue papers to create new colors. Some suggestions: magenta over yellow to create red; bright blue over yellow to create green; magenta over bright blue to create purple; combinations of all three to create black.

❹ Carefully lift off the tissue strips to reveal lovely lines of color. Which color combinations do you like or dislike? Do any of the color combinations result in a color that is different from what you expected?

water

gently lift

Try These Ideas!

■ If you know about the northern lights, or aurora borealis, use the tissue-paper strips to create a picture of those. Discuss where the northern lights can be seen, what colors they usually are, and what creates them.

■ Color Easter eggs by brushing each egg with a wet paintbrush. Place tissue papers on the eggs, then gently remove the tissue paper, and see the colored egg!

Tissue-Square Suncatchers

Tissue paper and liquid starch come together to catch the sun.

What You'll Need

black construction paper, 2 sheets

liquid starch

newspaper

paintbrushes

scissors

stapler

Styrofoam tray

tape

tissue paper (red, yellow, and orange)

wax paper

white crayons

Books to Enjoy

Catching the Sun by Coleen Paratore

The Sun Is My Favorite Star by Frank Asch

What to Do

1. Cut out many 1" squares of tissue paper in each color.
2. Spread newspaper on your work surface.
3. Carefully pour some liquid starch into the Styrofoam tray.
4. Cut a 9" x 12" piece of wax paper.
5. Paint starch onto half of the wax paper using a paintbrush. Arrange and place overlapping tissue squares on the starch to fill the area. Repeat on the other half of the wax paper. When finished with the tissue squares, the wax paper should be filled to 1"–2" from the edge.
6. Use the paintbrush to paint over the squares with more starch. Find a safe place where your work can dry overnight undisturbed.
7. Use a white crayon to draw the outline of a sun on one of the sheets of black paper.
8. Ask an adult to hold both sheets of black paper together while you cut the sun from the center, leaving the frame around the edges uncut.
9. Ask the adult to help you insert the decorated wax paper between the two black frames, and staple all three together.
10. Find a sunny window, and tape your picture to the window to catch the sun.

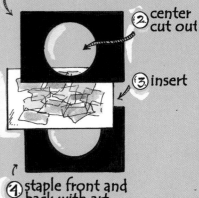

1. black construction paper
2. center cut out
3. insert
4. staple front and back with art in middle

57

Ribbon Weaving

Have fun with over and under!

What You'll Need

cardboard or stiff paper

fabric cut into strips,
1"–2" wide

lengths of ribbon in various
colors and widths

tape

Books to Enjoy

Abuela's Weave
by Omar S. Castaneda

Kente Colors
by Debbi Chocolate

Weaving the Rainbow
by George Ella Lyon

What to Do

1. Arrange lengths of ribbon or fabric in rows across the cardboard. How do the strips look and feel different from each other? Which ones are your favorites?
2. Tear off short strips of tape, and tape one end of each fabric strip to the cardboard.
3. Ask an adult to show you how to weave additional strips over and under the strips on the cardboard, going from side to side. Weave fabric and ribbons into the attached strips. Cloth is made by the process of weaving. Examine some of the fabric strips, and see if you can see how the fibers are woven together.
4. When you are finished, tear off more strips of tape, and tape the loose ends of the fabric strips and ribbons to the cardboard.

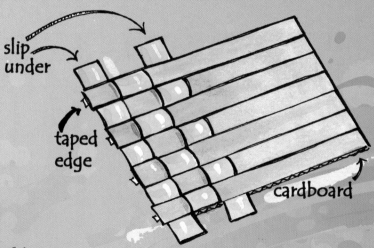

slip under

taped edge

cardboard

Try This!

Frame your weaving on a piece of black construction paper or poster board.

Tie-Dye Socks

Fabulous, funky footwear you make yourself!

What You'll Need

fabric dye, such as Rit®, in a variety of colors

latex (disposable) gloves

old shower curtain or large piece of heavy plastic

pair of white socks

pans or buckets to hold the dyes

rubber bands

Books to Enjoy

Gonna Like Me: Letting Off a Little Self-Esteem by Jamie Lee Curtis and Laura Cornell

I Want Your Moo by Marcella Bakur Weiner and Jill Neimark

The Yellow Tutu by Kirsten Bramsen

What to Do

1. Put on a paint smock or old shirt and, as a precaution, cover your work area with an old shower curtain or large piece of heavy plastic.

2. Ask an adult to put on latex gloves and mix up the dye according to package directions, if you are not using a premixed dye.

3. Ask an adult to show you how to twist rubber bands around your socks to create sections or patterns. Put the bands on as far apart or as close together as you would like. Try to make a different pattern on each sock. You also could tie knots in your socks to see what kind of effect that creates.

4. Put on rubber or latex gloves, and carefully pour different colors of dye into different pans or buckets.

5. Using the lightest color of dye first, swish either the whole sock or just part of the sock in one color dye. (The time needed for the sock to absorb the dye varies; follow the directions for your dye.)

6. Immerse the next section of the sock into the next-darkest dye (again, follow time recommendations!). What happens where the colors overlap? Did you expect this? Do you like the effect?

7. Continue with the next color of dye. Repeat with each sock, varying the patterns or colors as you want to.

8. Follow instructions for setting the dye. (This may require adult help or guidance.)

9. Wear your customized colorful socks with pride!

CHAPTER 6

Masterpieces and More

Sock Birds

Cereal Box Tote Bag

Homemade Paper Valentine

Soap Balls

Cookie-Cutter Wrapping Paper

Jeweled Eggs

Plaster Finger Puppets

Sock Birds

Turn old socks into your very own flock of birds.

What You'll Need

craft feathers

glue

googly eyes

scissors

socks, brightly colored

yellow felt

Books to Enjoy

About Birds: A Guide for Children
by Cathryn Sill

Owl Babies by Martin Waddell

The Plot Chickens
by Mary Jane Auch

What to Do

1. Lay a sock out flat so that you can see how and where to place the bird's features.
2. Cut a large, folded beak from the yellow felt to place inside of the sock bird's mouth at the end. (This may require adult help or guidance.)
3. Glue a pair of googly eyes on the sock.
4. Glue brightly colored feathers to the sock bird's head. You also can add feathers to the bottom of the sock for a feather-covered body.
5. Let the glue dry, then slide the sock onto your hand. Determine where the sock folds to make a "mouth."
6. Glue the yellow felt beak into the "mouth" area of the bird.

Try This!

Make up a story, and use the bird puppets to tell the story.

bright feathers

googly eyes

yellow felt

sock

Cereal Box Tote Bag

Recycle your cereal box and turn it into a fashionable tote.

What You'll Need

decorative items such as lace, buttons, and stickers

empty cereal box

glue thinned with water

hole punch

old magazines

paintbrush

ribbon or cord

scissors

Books to Enjoy

The Big Green Pocketbook
by Candice Ransom

I Need a Lunch Box
by Jeannette F. Caines

The Lady with the Alligator Purse
by Nadine Bernard Westcott

Lilly's Purple Plastic Purse
by Kevin Henkes

What to Do

1. Look through magazines, and cut out pictures of whatever appeals to you.
2. Take an empty cereal box and tuck in the flaps. Secure them with glue if necessary.
3. Use a hole punch to punch two holes in each side of the box.
4. Select a paintbrush, and use it to spread glue on both sides of the cereal box.
5. Arrange and apply the magazine pictures to the glued surface.
6. When you have finished putting pictures on the box, spread another coat of thinned glue over the entire box. Find a spot where the box can dry undisturbed.
7. Cut equal lengths of ribbon or cord; these will make the handles.
8. When the box is dry, thread the ribbon or cord through the holes. Make a knot on each end to secure it. Depending on your age and how nimble your fingers are, you may need an adult to do this step.
9. If you would like, add other objects to personalize your tote. You also could use it as a gift for someone.

Try These Ideas!

- Make a different tote for each season. Cover one tote with pictures of flowers for spring, one with pictures of leaves for fall, and so on.
- Create a tote with pictures in your favorite color or of your favorite animal.

Dog Tote

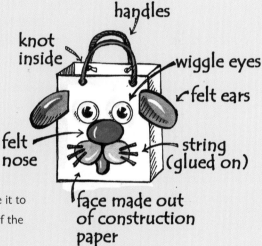

handles
knot inside
wiggle eyes
felt ears
felt nose
string (glued on)
face made out of construction paper

Homemade Paper Valentine

Show your love with a valentine you make from scratch.

What You'll Need

blender

framed screen that fits over a
bin, tub, or bucket

heart stencils

markers

measuring cup and water

newspaper

red food coloring

Books to Enjoy

*50 Simple Things Kids Can Do
to Save the Earth*
by The Earth Works Group

For the Love of Our Earth
by P. K. Hallinan

Guess How Much I Love You
by Sam McBratney

Just a Dream
by Chris van Allsburg

What to Do

1. Rip the newspaper into small pieces, as close to 1" x 2" as you can get. If necessary, ask an adult to rip up the first sheet, so you can see what size to aim for.

2. Place a handful or two of the torn paper into the blender. Fill a 1-cup measuring cup with water, and pour that and a few drops of red food coloring into the blender. Ask an adult to help you operate the blender and blend the paper into a pulp.

3. Place the screen over the bin, tub, or bucket. When the newspaper has finished blending, pour the mixture onto the screen. This lets the extra water drain.

4. Spread out the paper mixture over the screen to form a thin layer. Make sure there are no gaps in the mixture and that it lies smooth over the screen.

5. Allow the mixture to drip dry.

6. Place several pieces of newspaper over the mixture, and ask an adult to help you flip the screen over so that the red, recycled paper comes off the screen and lies on the newspaper. Move the stack to a warm spot where it can dry completely.

7. Trace a heart stencil on the homemade paper, and cut it out to make a valentine. If necessary, ask an adult for help with this step.

8. Give your paper heart to someone you love.

Try These Ideas!

- Make hearts in different colors.
- Use different stencils to make other shapes.

Soap Balls

Easy-to-make soap balls can be colored or scented and given as gifts.

What You'll Need

food coloring

laundry soap flakes

mixing bowls

spoon

tray or cookie sheet

vanilla or other scents (optional)

water

Books to Enjoy

My Five Senses by Aliki

Soap! Soap! Don't Forget the Soap! An Appalachian Folktale retold by Tom Birdseye

Soap, Soap, Soap/Jabon, Jabon, Jabon by Elizabeth O. Dulemba

What to Do

1. Pour soap flakes into bowls, using a separate bowl for each color you plan to use. **Hint:** If you cannot find soap flakes in your local store, find an online vendor. You can also create your own soap flakes by grating Ivory® soap bars on an old grater. You may need adult help with this.

2. Slowly add water to the flakes, and stir until the mixture is the consistency of very stiff dough. If you have trouble stirring, you can pour the water (carefully!) and ask an adult to stir.

3. Add drops of food coloring to each soap mixture, then mix the color into the soap. Add vanilla or other scents, if desired.

4. Scoop out a large spoonful of the soap mixture, and then shape it into a ball. Repeat until the soap mixture runs out. What does the soap mixture smell like? feel like? look like?

5. Place the balls onto the tray or cookie sheet, and find a spot where the balls won't get knocked around. Allow the balls to set and harden for two or three days.

6. Wash your hands with the soap balls at home or give them away as gifts.

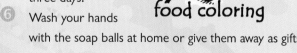

soap mixture

food coloring

cookie sheet

Try This!

Press the wet soap mixture into cookie-cutter shapes. Let the soap dry to make shaped soap.

Cookie-Cutter Wrapping Paper

Wrap your homemade gifts with wrapping paper you print yourself!

What You'll Need

large sheets of white butcher paper

liquid tempera paint, a variety of colors

plastic cookie cutters in various shapes

Styrofoam meat trays

tape

Books to Enjoy

The Elves and the Shoemaker by Paul Galdone

Harvey Slumfenburger's Christmas Present by John Burningham

Marvin's Best Christmas Present Ever by Katherine Paterson

What to Do

1. Pour just enough tempera paint in each tray to cover the bottom with a thin layer.
2. Select the cookie cutters that you like, and put one in each tray.
3. Get a piece of butcher paper. Print designs on the paper by dipping the cookie cutters in the paint and pressing them down on the paper. (You might want to print with the cookie cutter several times before returning it to the tray; otherwise, the prints could get blotchy and might smear.)
4. Try printing with different cookie cutters and paint colors. You can arrange the prints in a pattern or opt for a random design.
5. Repeat the process with more sheets of butcher paper. As you finish each sheet, move it to a safe location to dry.
6. When the wrapping papers have dried completely, voilà! You have wrapping paper for birthdays, the holidays, and any other occasion.

Jeweled Eggs

Long-ago rulers of Russia asked jewelers to make colorful jeweled eggs that usually held small surprises. Follow the tradition of Russian jewelers, and make your own beautiful jeweled eggs!

What You'll Need

glitter in rainbow colors

large plastic Easter eggs

paintbrushes

sequins

small paper cups

sturdy glue that bonds tightly to plastic

toothpicks

Books to Enjoy

Bunny Cakes by Rosemary Wells

First the Egg by Laura Vaccaro Seeger

The Odd Egg by Emily Gravett

What to Do

1. Put glue on the end of one large plastic egg, then fasten the egg securely to the bottom of a paper cup turned upside-down. Avoid using drinking cups that have wax on the outside, or the glue may not adhere to the cups.
2. Set the egg in a place where it can dry completely, and check on it from time to time to make sure it stays in place. Repeat the process with more eggs, if desired.
3. Cover your work area with newspaper (to catch any glue drips or extra glitter).
4. Use a paintbrush to paint glue on the egg. Add glitter and sequins to the eggs, however you would like. (Add the glitter to the eggs first, followed by sequins. Sequins can be put on individually using toothpicks to add dots of glue onto the backs of sequins.)
5. Let the eggs dry completely in an out-of-the-way spot. This may take some time and patience!

Try This!

Make this a treasure holder by decorating the top and bottom of the egg separately. Place a small treasure (shells, flowers, pretty rocks) inside the egg and add the top.

paint first (entire egg)

glue with glitter (rainbow colors)

sequins

painted circle

sequin

sequin

egg glued down

67

Plaster Finger Puppets

Experiment with plaster wrap to make puppets, and then put on a show.

What You'll Need

bowl of water

clay (optional)

glue

googly eyes

paint

paintbrush

petroleum jelly (optional)

plaster gauze or wrap, cut into 4" strips

yarn or doll hair (optional)

Book to Enjoy

My Apron by Eric Carle

What to Do

1. Pick a finger to "cast," then smear a small amount of petroleum jelly on that finger, if desired.
2. Dip the strips of plaster wrap into the bowl of water, and wrap them loosely around your finger, forming a cast. Ask an adult to help or guide you with this step.
3. Carefully remove the cast before it hardens. Find a safe place for the puppet to harden and dry.
4. After the cast dries, paint a face on it. If you want to attach hair and eyes, do so. Think about how everybody looks different. What colors of eyes and hair do your friends and family members have?
5. Attach some clay to the bases of the casts if you want the puppets to stand on their own.

yarn hair

googly eyes

Try This!

Create several puppets. Slide the puppets on your fingers, and then make up a story or choose a favorite story to act out.

Index

General Index